LEFT William Marshal
unhorses Baldwin de Guisnes.

RIGHT English Kings: above,
Henry II, Prince Henry (The
Young King) and Richard I
Lionheart; below, John and
Henry III.

This book ends with a
fascinating puzzle. The Rotunda of
the Temple Church still contains
eight 13th-century effigies of
knights in armour. Three of the
Marshals – William and two of his
sons – are known to have been
buried in the Church, and since
1843 one effigy in particular has
been universally accepted to be
William's. It is, as it should be, on
our front cover.

But now comes a query. A set of
drawings, c. 1610, has recently been
discovered in Washington, DC that
shows all the medieval effigies in
the Temple Church, and a further,
long-lost gravestone which matches
the earliest descriptions of
William's tomb. Has the real
monument to William been lost?
And has its appearance only now – after
hundreds of years – come back to light?

BELOW Henry II and his children.

William's Childhood and Adolescence

William's father John Marshal (1105–65) sided with Matilda in her ten years of civil war (1138–48) against King Stephen. William lived a perilous life from the start. At the age of five, he was a hostage in Stephen's hands. King Stephen besieged Newbury Castle, then held by William's father. The King granted a truce, to give time for the garrison to arrange a surrender. This was common practice, but John promptly used the truce to re-provision and fortify the garrison. In the face of such deception, young William's life was forfeit. Stephen threatened to kill the boy. William's father said he did not care, 'since he still had the anvils and hammers to forge even finer children.' Newbury Castle was worth more to him than William.

ABOVE Hamstead Marshall, probably the remains of the Marshal's motte and bailey castle.

By now William was in real danger. There was a first plan simply to hang him, then to launch him from a catapult over the castle's walls, and finally to tie him onto the wicker 'tortoise' carried for protection by platoons of troops as they approached a castle's walls. The castle's constable was not impressed. 'Do that,' he said, 'and I will drop a mill-stone on the shelter and flatten the boy like a pancake.' William was so innocently cheerful ('That's a new game! Dropping stones from the battlements!') that Stephen spared him. They ended up playing at soldiers, each with an army of plantain stalks.

William of Tancarville, 'a man noble in lineage, unique in war-craft, splendid in strength, the father of knights'

William's father is described in *The History* as *preudome corteis e sage*, 'a man of affairs, courtly and wise'. The *preudome* was an aristocratic ideal: judicious, mature and brave, with a dignity and integrity of his own. Unsurprisingly, Stephen's side described him less kindly, as 'a limb of hell and root of all evil', who built castles without permission and robbed both clergy and laity of their land. Either way, everyone agreed that he was a man of great cunning and endless stratagems.

William himself will have set out to be, and undoubtedly became, a perfect *preudome*. He was lucky – and determined – in making the right connections. At 13 he was sent to Normandy to the household of William of Tancarville, described as 'a man noble in lineage, unique in war-craft, splendid in strength, the father of knights', to learn the ways of a knight. (There is a story, probably told by William himself, that he was known at Tancarville only for being a greedy-guts.) On his return to England, William went straight to his mother's brother, Patrick Earl of Salisbury, and entered the Earl's household. William was making his way in the world.

BELOW The Castle of Tancarville.

Eleanor of Aquitaine

Twelfth-century England was a man's world, and in telling William's story we are inevitably telling the stories of the great men around him. But three women were pivotal in his life, every one of them extraordinary in her own right. The first was Eleanor of Aquitaine. Eleanor was one of the great heiresses of Europe: her territory of Aquitaine was a large part of south-west France, fertile and rich. She first married King Louis VII of France, who badly needed her land and resources to bolster his small kingdom and secure his Capetian dynasty. In 1152 their marriage was annulled, and within weeks Eleanor had married Louis's

ABOVE Royal Procession, early 13th century, Chinon, France: in the lead, Henry II; in the centre, crowned, Eleanor of Aquitaine.

bitter rival, Henry II of England. Henry's Angevin empire now stretched almost 1,000 miles from the Scottish borders to the Pyrenees.

The nobles of Aquitaine felt no loyalty to Henry. To secure control, in 1168, Henry and Eleanor both went to Aquitaine. Henry summoned Patrick Earl of Salisbury to be his second-in-command, and with Patrick went his young nephew, William. Disaster followed: local nobles ambushed the Queen and her party. Patrick and his troops, badly outnumbered, covered the Queen's escape. Patrick was killed; the furious William charged, was badly wounded and was captured. But Eleanor surely heard of William's ferocious courage. She ransomed him and took him into her household. William's new patron was the most powerful woman in Europe, wife to the King of England and of half France.

TOURNAMENTS

'This Way! Over here! God save the Marshal!'

William grew up, we are told, to be tall, well-proportioned and handsome, with brown hair and complexion, and with a broad stride that suited him perfectly for riding.

Tournaments were the epitome of chivalric life and a perfect training for battle. For a large tournament, nobles would gather from far and wide with their entourage or *mesnie*. The Chamberlain of Tancarville, for instance, might well have 30 knights under his banner; great nobles such as Henry the Young King (who will

ABOVE *The Book of the Tournament of René d'Anjou*, c. 1460: The competitors are gathered.

play a large part in William's story) might well bring 80–100. Well over 200 mounted knights could be gathered, overall. Foot-soldiers and archers could be taking part too.

A large area was marked out by palisades and ditches; it could include whole villages and their fields. (All were in danger of serious damage, so Richard I Lionheart specified just five places in England where tournaments could legally be held). Within the area were *recets*, refuges where knights could honourably rest or rearm without being attacked. The gathered forces were divided into two teams according to their regions of origin or political allegiances.

One team charged in serried ranks with lances extended, and the *mêlée* began: with lances and – when these were broken – with swords and maces. Tournaments could be fought *à plaisance* (with blunted weapons) or *à l'outrance* (with sharpened); when *à plaisance*, no booty or ransom, it seems, could be taken. Both forms involved ferocious fighting and

'I've captured five hundred knights and kept their arms, their horses and all their gear. If that means the Kingdom of Heaven is closed to me, then that's that – I can't give them back!'

demanded severe courage and coolness. Only three things distinguished tournaments from real battles: knights were to be captured, not killed, there were *recets*, and prisoners must be released. (Even in battle, it was far preferable – and far more profitable – to capture and ransom an enemy knight than to kill him.)

Knights in a tournament who were captured by an opponent had to leave the field and arrange their ransom. Horses and armour were booty for the captor. (Accounts were settled at the end of the day; a knight could agree his own ransom and then rejoin the *mêlée*.) That team won who held the field at the day's end or who commanded the greater booty and ransoms.

As a young man, William was famed for his own fighting and for his leadership in these staged battles. Even at his first tournament, he won four war-horses, a string of palfreys and packhorses, and a fine array of equipment. In early tournaments he could be too rash, but he learnt that discipline and a tight formation

were vital if a cohort of knights was to be successful. Such a group could profitably surround and capture a single opponent, or could join late in the fray – as William learnt to do – when most of the combatants were already tired and disorganized.

William became, in effect, a team-captain and manager on the international and professionalized tournament-circuit, and he won from it immense prestige, booty and ransom-money – and keen followers. Henry the Northerner, surely a herald-at-arms, was well-known for shouting out in tournaments, 'This way! Over here! God save the Marshal!'

On his deathbed, William was advised, in order to be forgiven his sins, to return all the possessions to the knights from whom he had taken them. William protested: 'The clergy are too hard on us. They shave us too close! I've captured five hundred knights and kept their arms, their horses and all their gear. If that means the Kingdom of Heaven is closed to me, then that's that – I can't give them back!' *The History* is a rumbustious record of William's tournaments and of the admiration and money he won from them. William's own estimate of his successes is probably too low. *The History*'s author had access to the records of William's tournaments over a period of just nine months, in which William and a companion Roger de Gaugy captured 103 knights. The author thought Roger was too greedy, but he knew how valuable the captives' ransoms, horses and equipment were to William.

ABOVE *The Book of the Tournament of René d'Anjou*: The tournament.

OPPOSITE *The Book of the Tournament of René d'Anjou*: Combat.

A LANCELOT IN REAL LIFE
William and the Romances

The History already belonged, when it was written in the 1220s, in a rich confusion of history, poetry and legend. Its William is a 'real-life' Lancelot. It can be difficult at times to know whether art was imitating life, or life art. *The History* tells of tournaments fought in the 1170s. Prominent at such tournaments had been Count Philip of Flanders. Philip was patron of the greatest poet of the age, Chrétien de Troyes. Chrétien may even have seen some of the tournaments in which William himself took part. Philip would gladly have been William's patron too: he offered William the vast transfer-fee and retainer of 500 pounds a year to enter his service.

In his poems, Chrétien transformed the acquisitive, mercenary knights of William's day into chivalric ideals who thought only of honour and prowess. By the time *The History* was written, Chrétien's poems had swept through Northern Europe. *The History* has one gracious story of a tournament at Pleurs from which William won great honour but no booty at all – until he was awarded a pike, presented to the tournament's leaders by a noblewoman and passed on by general acclaim to the knight who had fought to best effect. That knight was William, who was found in the smithy having his dented helmet removed by the smith.

One of the great modern scholars of William describes him in his early years as a mercenary bully. We can see why! ('How much you've got,' remarks *The History*, 'is how much you're worth – and how much we care about you!') It is all the more striking that by the time he was an old man, he was his country's greatest statesman.

LEFT Angoulême, France, c. 1130: The Battle of Roncevalle.

ABOVE The Siege of the Castle of Love, ivory casket, c. 1340, Paris.

BELOW Albert of Rapperswil jousting.

'GIVE ME A GOOD HORSE, MARSHAL!'

One of William's early tournaments was at Joigny. For the first time, we hear of noblewomen being present. This was a motif already familiar, when *The History* was written, in Chrétien's poetry. 'The ladies,' we hear in *The History*, 'redoubled the strength, the spirit, the courage and the heart of every knight present.' While William's company was waiting for the opponents to muster their forces, 'a young singer, a novice herald-of-arms' struck up a new song. Its refrain included, 'Give me a good horse, Marshal!' The herald wanted a real destrier, a war-horse, instead of a mere palfrey. William heard the song, mounted his own horse, told the singer to follow him, charged some opposing knights, seized a horse, threw off its rider and gave it to the singer. The herald mounted and they rejoined their own company before they had even been missed. Now the herald was singing, 'Look, look, what a horse! The Marshal gave it to me!'

9

WILLIAM AND THE YOUNG KING
'Finest of all Princes on Earth'

King Henry II crowned his own eldest surviving son, the younger Henry, in 1170. William, several years older than this Young King Henry and already famous, was placed in his retinue to guard and instruct him.

In 1182, William's position was suddenly and deeply endangered. He was accused of having an affair with the Young King's wife, Margaret of France. (There was a second, and perhaps better founded, accusation: that he was tactless at best – and seriously insubordinate at worst – to have adapted the great war-cry of the Norman kings, *Dex aïe*, 'God my help!', to become his own, *Dex aïe li Mareschal*, 'God help the Marshal!') *The History* tells the story at length. We hear – with an angry play on their names – of the principal slanderers, Norman-French members of the Young King's entourage who were jealous of the English William's success and growing renown: Adam d'Yquebeuf, who beefed up the story, 'a foul brew in a foul vessel'; Sir Thomas de Coulonces, who 'added his two ounces of salt, all he was good for';

and the young Ralph Farci ('Stuffed'), in favour with the Young King. The chief conspirators got Farci drunk, 'stuffed' him with the story, and sent him off to tell the Young King.

William's response to the charge was typical. At Christmas 1182, he went to the Kings' court to clear his name. He offered to fight the three accusers on three successive days, and before the fights – if the Young King so determined – to have a finger cut off his right

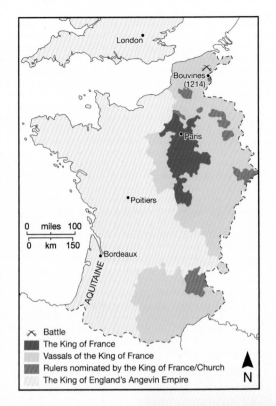

OUTWITTING THE MARSHAL

At a tournament with the Young King Henry at Anet, William and Henry found themselves alone, confronting 300 foot-soldiers under Simon de Neauphle. William, of course, charged straight at them; they ran away, and William grabbed de Neauphle's horse by the bridle. As he led back the captured horse and rider, de Neauphle saw an overhanging gutter, grabbed it and was left behind in mid-air as William, all unawares, led his horse onwards. The Young King watched the whole incident unfold. Back at the baggage-train, William ordered his groom to take charge of the captive knight. The Young King laughed out loud: 'Which knight would that be?' This must have been a favourite story of William's, told against himself.

ABOVE The Angevin Empire of the English kings, c. 1200.

LEFT The marriage of Margaret, widow of the Young King, to the king of Hungary.

RIGHT Coronet worn by Margaret at her wedding to the Young King. Margaret's dowry was the vital territory of Vexin, west of Paris.

hand. If he lost any of the fights, the Young King could hang him on the spot. It is hardly a surprise that nobody took up his challenge. Impetuous, forthright and reliant on his patent prowess in battle: all this is William to the core.

And in the ritualized extravagance of his challenge, we are once more in the world of the Arthurian and Grail romances. Life and literature, chivalry and romance – we are in a hall of mirrors here.

William on Crusade

I n 1183 William was in the service of the Young King when the Young King died. Young King Henry had vowed to go on Crusade, and William discharged his lord's vow by going on Crusade himself. He spent two years in the Holy Land. While there, he entrusted his body, wherever he should die, to the Knights Templar for burial among them.

The crusades were the epitome of feudal life. The great liege-lord of all knights was Christ. His home and honour were under threat from his enemies; his knights must rally in their Lord's defence. Most devoted of all his household were those such as the Templars who were both men of prayer and men of war. (The combination was as strange then as it would be now.) The Templars were also famously brave and disciplined in battle. William will have learnt much from them.

He also acquired two lengths of silk which he brought back with him from the Holy Land. They were to cover his coffin, when he died. When they were brought out for use, 30 years later, they were slightly faded, but were 'of the finest, most exquisite work'. After his funeral (and protected from the rain, if it were a wet day), they were to be given to the Templars to use as they wished.

BELOW A city under siege, ivory, 12th century, French.

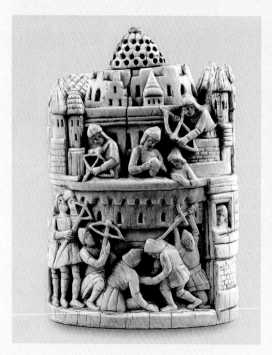

SIR JESUS AND THE JOUST

Easier to organize than the tournament, and more exciting to watch, was the joust. Jousting was so familiar that the poet William Langland (c. 1380), in his allegorical poem *Piers Plowman*, describes the climactic battle between Christ and the Devil as a joust between the two. Faith, like a herald, arranges the combatants. 'Will', the poem's speaker and a personification of human will, dreams of Palm Sunday in Jerusalem, when Jesus entered the city on an ass. Will sees a man approach who resembles both the Good Samaritan and the honest ploughman Piers himself. The man

Bare-foot on an ass's back bootless came riding,
Without spurs or spear lively he looked,
As is known in a knight that draws near to be dubbed
To get him gilt spurs or slashed shoes.

Then Faith, framed in a window, cried, 'Come! Son of David!'
Like a herald at arms when adventurers come jousting.
Then I found out from Faith what meant this affair,
And who would joust in Jerusalem: 'Jesus,' he said,
'And will win what the Fiend wants, Piers Plowman for food.
Jesus in his gentility will joust in Piers' arms,
In his helmet and hauberk – human nature itself.'
'Who shall joust against Jesus,' I asked, 'Jews or scribes?'
No,' said Faith; 'but the Fiend and falsehood and death.'

Jesus has become a would-be knight, coming to prove himself in the lists. Every knight going, as William did, to Jerusalem could see himself in this heroic figure.

LEFT Crusading knight kneeling in prayer.

ABOVE A battle in the crusades.

William and Richard Lionheart

I n 1188–89 William campaigned with Henry II against the King of France. Henry's son Prince Richard sided with the French. In a skirmish, William unhorsed Richard and could have killed him, but instead killed Richard's horse. Within days Henry II had died. The new King Richard summoned William, and to save face insisted that he, Richard, had saved his own life in the encounter: 'Marshal, the other day, you intended to kill me, and you would have if I had not deflected your lance with my arm.' William bravely – or rashly – held his ground: 'I never intended to kill you. I am strong enough to aim my lance, and if I had wanted, I could have killed you.' It must have been a tense moment, but it won for William the new King's respect. Richard sent William to England to secure all the King's interests and to take a secret message to the King's mother, Eleanor of Aquitaine. Her patronage of the young William, 20 years before, had borne good fruit: he was becoming a power in the land.

Richard confirmed William's marriage to Isabel de Clare, daughter of the late Richard Strongbow, Earl of Pembroke, and of the Irish princess Aoife (Eve) of Leinster. Isabel was born soon after 1170. She was heiress of vast lands in Ireland, England, France and Wales. She was taken into the King's custody in England and the King, as her guardian, could decide whom she was to marry. She was a teenager when in 1189 she was married to William, who was over 20 years older than her.

William was one of four co-justiciars appointed to protect King Richard's realm in England while the King was on Crusade. He went to Vézeley to see the King set off on 4 July 1190. William remained loyal, even when rumours were spread that the King was dead, and William's own older brother sided with the King's scheming brother John.

> *'I never intended to kill you. I am strong enough to aim my lance, and if I had wanted I could have killed you.'*

WILLIAM'S HIGH WORTH

William had a sure sense of his own worth.
We have a letter to him from Henry II, 1188,
summoning William to fight in France against
King Philip of France, who had attacked
Châteauroux.

*I request that you come to me fully equipped
as soon as may be, with as many knights as
you can get, to support me in my war. You
have ever so often moaned to me that I have
bestowed on you a small fee. Know for sure
that if you serve me faithfully I will give you
in addition Châteauroux with all its lordship
and whatever belongs to it as soon as we may
be able.*

This was a promise of more than land and
income. William had been due to marry
Heloise of Lancaster; the King was now
promising him the richer prize of Denise of
Châteauroux. In the following months, the
arrangements were changed again: William's
friend Baldwin of Béthune was given Denise,
and William was promised the far greater
heiress Isabel, daughter and heir of Earl
Richard of Striguil (Chepstow).

ABOVE Richard I Lionheart, by Carlo
Marochetti (1805-67), Palace of
Westminster.

BELOW Richard I Lionheart, disguised
as a pilgrim, at his capture.

ABOVE Richard I Lionheart's Great Seal.

LEFT The coronation of Richard I Lionheart.

A SECOND HEROINE
Isabel of Clare

Isabel's grandfather Diarmait Mac Murchada made an alliance with Richard Strongbow for the recovery of Mac Murchada's kingdom in Leinster. Henry II had stripped Strongbow of his lands as Earl of Pembroke; here was the chance to remake his fortune. To seal the alliance, Diarmait's daughter Aoife was married to Strongbow. At Diarmait's death, Strongbow came into possession of all his wife's lands.

The Lords of Leinster had no reason to value William, but Isabel could command real loyalty. The period 1207–8 was a testing time: parts of Leinster were in rebellion against William, encouraged by King John's justiciar

Meiler fitz Henry, and John ordered William himself back to England. Isabel was clearly prominent in the debate that followed; she distrusted John's intentions. *The History* has William, before setting off, address his lords dramatically in Kilkenny, with Isabel, heavily pregnant, beside him:

'My lords, here you see the countess whom I have brought here by the hand into your presence. She is your lady by birth, the daughter of the Earl who graciously, in his generosity, gave you all your fiefs when he had conquered the land. She stays behind here with you as a pregnant woman, until such time as God brings me back here. I ask you all to give her unreservedly the protection she deserves by birthright; for she is your lady, as we well know. I have no claim to anything here except through her.'

With William gone to England, Meiler besieged Kilkenny Castle. Far from surrendering, Isabel had a man lowered from the battlements to alert her allies to the crisis. The siege was raised, and Meiler was thoroughly humiliated. Isabel made him submit to her personally, and took his son hostage for future good behaviour. She also took the sons or brothers of other rebellious lords, and – according to *The History* – was extremely displeased when William, on his return to Ireland, forgave the rebels and released the hostages: 'they had done Isabel many a wrong; had William listened to her, he would have exacted revenge on them.'

Here was a redoubtable countess, well worthy of her husband. All the more poignant is *The History*'s account of her when William died: 'the countess could not walk without danger of coming to grief, for her heart and body, her head and limbs had suffered from her exertions, her weeping and her vigils.'

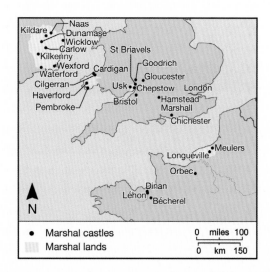

ABOVE The lands of William Marshal and the Countess of Pembroke.

OPPOSITE *The Marriage of Richard Strongbow and Aoife* by Daniel Maclise (painted 1854).

BELOW Chepstow Castle. In the 1190s, William built the new gatehouse and added round towers to the Middle Bailey.

CHRONOLOGY
The Life and Times of William Marshal

c. 1147 William born, second son of John Marshal and Sibyl of Salisbury

1152 King Stephen besieges Newbury Castle; William a hostage, and threatened with death

1154 Accession of King Henry II

c. 1160 William to Tancarville, Normandy, to train as a knight

1165 Death of William's father

1166 William knighted; his first battle at Neufchâtel; his first tournament, near Le Mans

1168 William to Aquitaine in retinue of Patrick of Salisbury; wounded and captured by the Lusignans; ransomed by Eleanor of Aquitaine; enters Eleanor's retinue

1170 Coronation of Henry, the Young King; William appointed the Young King's tutor-in-arms

1173–74 First rebellion against Henry II, by Henry the Young King

1176 The Young King and William start touring the tournaments in Northern France

1179 William raises his own banner at tournament at Lagny-sur-Marne

1180 Accession of King Philip II Augustus of France

1182 William accused of an affair with Margaret, wife of the Young King; forced into exile. Goes to shrine of the Three Kings (the Magi of the Christmas story) in Cologne, probably to ask their prayers for his own standing with his two earthly kings

1183 Second rebellion against Henry II. William returns to the Young King's retinue. The Young King dies; William sets out for the Holy Land to discharge the Young King's vow. He probably returns when the Lusignans gain control of Jerusalem

c. 1186 William enters the household of King Henry II

1187 The Battle of Hattin: Saladin defeats the Crusaders

and captures Jerusalem; the Third Crusade begins

1189 William unhorses Prince Richard Lionheart at Le Mans. Accession of King Richard Lionheart. William marries Isabel of Clare, heiress of Striguil (Chepstow)

1190–94 King Richard away on Crusade and in captivity. William as co-justiciar of England. Death of William's elder brother John, 1194

1194–99 William fighting alongside King Richard

1199 King Richard killed at Châlus. Accession of King John. William appointed Earl of Pembroke

1200 Treaty of Le Goulet between King John and Philip II Augustus

1200–1 William visits Pembroke and Ireland for first time

1202 William defends Normandy from the French. King John relieves Mirebeau

1203 King John (probably) murders his nephew Prince Arthur of Brittany

1204 King John loses Normandy, Anjou and Poitou to the French

1205 King John quarrels with William

1207–8 William returns to Ireland. The crisis in Leinster

1210 King John leads an expedition to Ireland against William de Briouze

1212 Plot to assassinate King John. William returns to the King's favour

May–July 1213 King John submits to the Pope. The King stays at the Templars' house near Dover. William is witness and guarantor of the King's submission. The King's excommunication is lifted; in return, he offers a golden mark borrowed from the Master of the Temple

27 July 1214 King John is defeated at the Battle of Bouvines and loses all hope of recovering his French possessions

16–23 November 1214 The King is in the Temple. On 21 November, he issues from the Temple the charter granting 'with the common consent of our barons' free elections to cathedral and conventual churches, and on 22 November, a grant to St Paul's Cathedral

7–15 January 1215 The King is in the Temple. A group of barons confronts him with demands. John gives the barons a safe conduct until after Easter; William Marshal and the Archbishop are among the King's guarantors, assuring the barons that the King will then give them satisfaction. On 15 January, the cathedral and convent charger of 21 November 1214 is reissued from the Temple

16–22 April 1215 (Eastertide) The King is in the Temple

7–9 May 1215 The King is in the Temple. On 9 May, the charter is issued from the Temple that guarantees to the City of London the right freely to elect its own Lord Mayor

17 May 1215 The barons capture London. The balance of power now lies against the King; he must negotiate

28 May 2015 The King receives the imperial regalia of his grandmother, the Empress Matilda, from the custody of the Master of the Temple. He is going to assert his full majesty at the coming negotiations

10 June 1215 The King arrives at Runnymede

15 June 1215 The King seals the Charter. William and Brother Aymeric, Master of the Temple, are listed among those who have advised the King. William's eldest son is one of the 'Twenty-Five'

Surety Barons, appointed to ensure the King's conformity to the Charter's terms

19 October 1216 King John dies. The King's Council names William the Guardian (Rector) of the young King Henry III and of the realm

12 November 1216 William reissues the Charter under his own seal

20 May 1217 Battle of Lincoln

24 August 1217 Battle of Sandwich

6 November 1217 William again reissues the Charter under his own seal. Particular clauses are removed and issued separately as the Charter of the Forest; the remaining reissued clauses from 1215 are now known as the Great Charter (Magna Carta)

14 May 1219 William dies at Caversham, and is buried on 20 May in the Temple's Round Church

1224 William Marshal the Younger, 2nd Earl of Pembroke, marries Eleanor, sister of King Henry III

c. 1226 *The History* is completed

MAGNA CARTA, 1215
William Marshal, Hero of the Hour

Immediately after his coronation in 1199, King John invested William with the sword of office as Earl of Pembroke. There followed over ten troubled years, several spent in Ireland, as William rose and fell in the King's favour.

The trouble started in 1204–5. William had lands in France for which he owed fealty to King Philip of France, not to King John. By 1205 King Philip (it seems) demanded that William acknowledge Philip as William's only liege-lord on the continent. William would then be unable ever to fight there against Philip on John's behalf. William accepted.

This was brinkmanship at best. John accused him of treachery. William characteristically offered to fight anyone in single combat who thought him a traitor – and none of John's knights dared take up the challenge. John took William's eldest son as hostage instead. In 1208 John demanded William's second son, Richard, as well.

Only in 1212 was William's position once more secure, when he extracted from 26 Anglo-

LEFT The Unknown Charter, probably drawn up at the Temple, London, January 1215.

BELOW The Temple, London, from the air.

Irish barons new oaths of allegiance to John. In exchange, John released his hostages, and in 1213, ordered William himself to return from Leinster to England. William, already in his mid-sixties, was with a handful of others about to determine the whole future of England.

William was at the centre of negotiations between John and the barons, 1214–15. He was at the Temple in London when the barons came to a conference there in January 1215 'fully armed and ready for war'. According to the barons' account, they asked the King to confirm their ancient and accustomed liberties; he refused, and in turn, he asked them to undertake in writing on behalf of themselves and their successors that they would never in future demand such liberties. Now the barons refused. John sought refuge in delay. Such innovation, he

said, would take time. The barons gave him warning: they were pledging themselves, one and all, as a wall of defence for the house of the Lord and would stand firm for the liberty of the Church and the realm. The barons rightly distrusted the King; during the negotiations, John sent emissaries (surely secretly) to the Pope.

A charter rediscovered only in 1863, now known as the Unknown Charter, probably

LEFT **King John's disastrous defeat at the Battle of Bouvines, 27 July 1214, painted by Horace Vernet (1789–1863).**

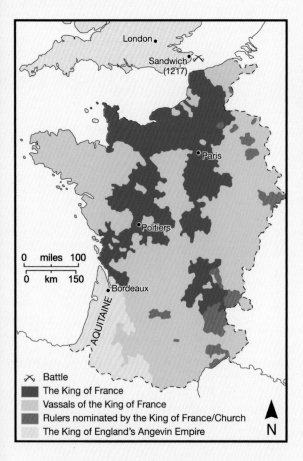

Map legend:

0 miles 100
0 km 150

⚔ Battle
■ The King of France
□ Vassals of the King of France
■ Rulers nominated by the King of France/Church
□ The King of England's Angevin Empire

N

LEFT The Angevin Empire of the English kings after Bouvines.

William and Langton were again sent to appease them. On 5 May, the rebel barons renounced their fealty to the King and the country was on the brink of civil war. The King had the Pope and all apparent right on his side. A fair part of the baronage was at worst neutral, at best loyal to John, and on 9 May, from the Temple, John sought the vital support of London by granting its free governance.

To Runnymede – and beyond

The King must have thought himself well prepared. But on 17 May the rebels captured London and the balance of power moved suddenly and irrevocably against John. He sent William to London to tell the rebel barons that he was ready to negotiate. When agreement was at last reached at Runnymede on 15 June, William was named first among the magnates who had advised the King.

So the Great Charter came into being. And within it two rights are granted that have never been forgotten or superseded:

'No free person shall be taken or imprisoned or dispossessed or outlawed or exiled or in any way ruined, nor will we go or send against him except by the lawful judgement of his equals or by the law of the land. To no one will we sell, to no one will we deny or delay right or justice.'

records the terms of the barons' demands in January 1215. First, 'King John concedes that he will not take a man without judgment, or accept anything for doing justice and will not do injustice.' This was a guarantee which the barons badly needed, right at the start: that the following demands would not, in themselves, bring down the King's retribution. Then the charter turns from 'he' to 'I', for the King's further undertakings. The authority of the 'counsel/council of the barons' is written into the charter. This would become a central component of Magna Carta: a genuine, enforceable check on the King's executive power.

It was William and Archbishop Langton who pledged on the king's behalf that he would meet the barons again in April. By the end of April, the barons realized that John had no intention of yielding. They applied pressure by besieging Brackley in Northamptonshire;

A powerful king could, of course, ignore such terms. But at the Charter's end, all the rights that it granted were guaranteed by dramatic and enforceable restraints imposed on the King's power. Twenty-five barons were charged to enforce the King's conformity to the Charter; among them was William Marshal II, the Earl's eldest son.

The barons' success was unsustainable; under the guise of fealty, they had all but dethroned a king. John soon sought to repudiate the Charter: it had, he said, been sealed under duress from barons who had made themselves the judges in their own cause. (He had a point.) No wonder the King appealed to Rome to have the Charter annulled – and no wonder the Pope granted his request. In September 1215, Pope Innocent III annulled this 'shameful and demeaning agreement, forced upon the King by violence and fear'.

The Charter joined the host of other failed charters of the Middle Ages, annulled or unenforced. It was sinking without trace; until William Marshal revived, revised and reissued it in his plan to save the country.

23

WILLIAM MARSHAL
Regent of the King and of the Realm, 1216–19

The rebel barons soon realized that the King would resist any attempt to enforce the Charter. William's son William Marshal II had sided, as we have seen, with these barons. On 10 May 1216, Aymeric de St Maur, Master of the Temple in England and a close ally of the Marshals, escorted the younger William under safe passage to see his father. They had much to plan. A family 'de Saint Maur' was prominent in Wiltshire, William's home-county; Aymeric and the Marshals may have known each other all their lives.

The rebels were turning to the French king

RIGHT Magna Carta, 1216: the only copy known to survive, in Durham Cathedral.

RIGHT The second Coronation of
King Henry III (born 1207, reigned
1216–72), in Westminster Abbey, 1220.

for help, and on 21 May 1216, Prince
Louis of France landed with his army
at Thanet in Kent. The younger
William declared his allegiance to the
French and was confirmed as the
'Marshal' of Prince Louis' court.
With the rebels' help, the French
quickly occupied London and most
of eastern England.

King John drew up a hurried will.
He entrusted his son Henry to
thirteen overseers, among them
William. The King died, 19 October
1216. His son Henry was only nine
years old. Half the boy's supposed
kingdom was in the hands of the
French, the treasury was empty, the
rebels were on the march. The few
barons who had remained loyal to
John and to his son had good reason
to abandon Henry to his fate. But
enough stayed firm – and chief
among them was William. After
short consultations, William agreed
to become Guardian of the King and
of the Realm.

'I have ventured into the wild sea,'
said William to his own close advisors,
'where even the most experienced sailors
find no shore nor
anchorage. But if all the
world had abandoned the
King except me, I would
put him on my shoulders
and carry him without
fail from island to island,
from land to land, even if I had to beg for
bread!'

William had to win back the barons'
allegiance. In a brilliant stroke, he and the
Papal Legate reissued Magna Carta in
November 1216. This new issue was written in
Henry's name but was 'given by the hands' of
the Legate and William; they sealed and so

*'I have ventured into the
wild sea, where even the
most experienced sailors find
no shore nor anchorage.'*

guaranteed it, since young Henry did not yet
have a seal of his own. The demands of the
rebels, so fiercely resisted by John, were now
being met, at Henry's own
initiative, by the boy-king.
The enforcement clause,
which had made the 1215
Charter so inflammatory,
was omitted; the Charter
was, from now on, to be a
conservative, sustainable document.

In this issue, the Charter of 1215 had been
skilfully adapted. The new version admitted
that the old had in it 'weighty and doubtful'
matters which must be left in abeyance for now
until Henry could take further counsel and
then do what was best for 'the common utility
of all'.

25

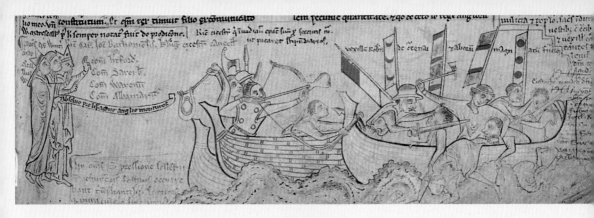

'THIS WAY! GOD IS WITH THE MARSHAL!'

Saving England at the Battle of Lincoln, 1217

In the spring of 1217, the fortunes of Henry III began to improve. The 1216 Charter was working: it remedied the complaints which had led to the barons' rebellion. Rebel barons realized the danger that Louis would eventually reward his own retainers and not them. On 5 March, the great William Longsword, Earl of Salisbury, returned to Henry's side and brought with him the younger William Marshal.

But the enemy still occupied most of eastern England. From early March, the city of Lincoln was in French hands, and the castle itself was under siege. Early in May, Prince Louis of France divided his own forces in two: he himself led a siege of Dover, and sent the rest of the army north to strengthen the siege of Lincoln.

William, now nearly 70 years old, decided to venture everything on a single battle at Lincoln before Louis could reunite his forces.

He led the loyalist army, in person, into battle. Impetuous as ever, he set off without a helmet. An esquire pointed this out; William duly put one on and then rushed into the fray, we are told, like a merlin, sparrowhawk or lion. William directed the battle with tactical brilliance and to overwhelming victory.

The 46 English barons on the rebels' side and over 300 unnamed knights simply surrendered. The rebellion within England was over. The French still had one further move to make: an attempt to reinforce Prince Louis in his siege of Dover. William rode rapidly south to Sandwich, equipped a fleet, and on 24 August watched as the French ships were captured, sunk or put to flight. The war had ended at last; Henry III was safe on his throne.

ABOVE The Battle of Sandwich, 24 August 1217.

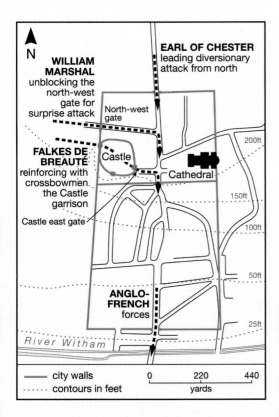

ABOVE The Battle of Lincoln, 20 May 1217.

RIGHT Lincoln Castle.

A THIRD HEROINE: NICOLA DE LA HAIE AT LINCOLN CASTLE

Nicola was hereditary castellan of Lincoln Castle. She remained stalwartly loyal to John as Prince and then King. On the very day of his death, the King appointed her joint Sheriff of Lincolnshire. John's confidence was well placed. In March 1217, the French army under Gilbert de Gant attacked Lincoln. The city surrendered quickly, but Nicola knew exactly how to hold the Castle. Her garrison held out against Gilbert and then against the reinforcements from Louis under the Comte de Perche. Siege machinery bombarded the castle all through March, April and early May. William saw the danger mounting, assembled

an army at Newark and marched on the city. Nicola's deputy showed William an entrance, blocked up and forgotten, in the city's wall through which his army could pour into the city and take the French by surprise. Most contemporary chroniclers admired her greatly. They were uncertain how to praise a woman who proved herself such a formidable warrior. She was, we read, a noble woman who acted manfully and thought of nothing womanly. Only one chronicler, devoted to the French cause, spoke ill of her: as 'a very cunning, bad-hearted and vigorous old woman'. But he had good reason to resent her!

William Marshal's Last Years

In November 1217, William issued and sealed Magna Carta yet again, this time as two separate charters. He was concentrating now on the correction of King John's abuses. A third of England was under the King's control as royal forest. Successive kings had 'afforested' ever larger areas, as much to generate revenue as to use for hunting. The penalties for infringing the King's rights were severe. In 1217 William removed from the Great Charter all the clauses connected with the royal forests, and issued them as a separate charter, the Charter of the Forest. Vast tracts of land were to be 'disafforested' or removed from the royal forest. The terms of this charter could never be fully met, but they united the country behind Henry. William was unravelling one of the most notorious and deeply resented abuses of recent reigns.

Within eighteen months, William's health was fading. On his deathbed at Caversham, William summoned Brother Aymeric, Master of the Temple, to prepare for William's own admission to the Templars. William's almoner Geoffrey, a Templar, brought him the Templar cloak which had secretly been made for him a year before. William had arranged to be buried in front of the rood-screen in the Temple Church. Aymeric predeceased the sick Marshal by just a few days, having asked to be buried next to him: 'For I greatly loved his company on earth; may God grant that we be companions in heaven.'

The silks William had brought back from the Holy Land, 30 years before, duly covered the coffin at his funeral. It is a measure of William's achievement that his cortège was led to the Temple Church by former rebels, now pacified. The Archbishop of Canterbury and the Bishop of London presided when William was laid to rest here on 20 May 1219. The Archbishop said:

'You see before you the greatest knight of the world that ever lived in our time, and what is there to say now, by God?'

'Look, sirs, how it is with this life: when each of us comes to his end his senses are all gone, and he is nothing more than so much earth. You see before you the greatest knight of the world that ever lived in our time, and what is there to say now, by God? This is what we all must come to. We have before us our mirror; it is mine as much as yours. And now let us say the Our Father, praying that God may receive this Christian in His heavenly kingdom, in glory with His elect, believing as we do, that he was truly good.'

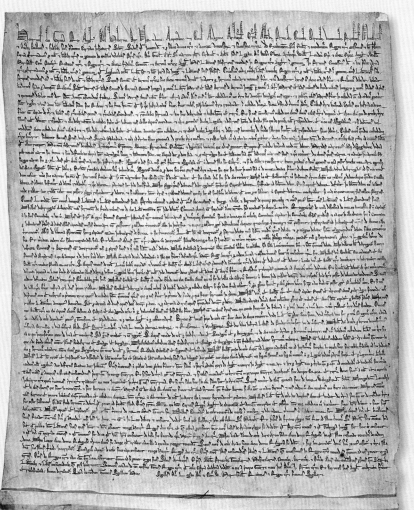

LEFT Magna Carta, 1217, with the modest seal (right), which William always retained, of a mere household knight.

RIGHT The Charter of the Forests, 1217.

WILLIAM MARSHAL IN THE TEMPLE CHURCH

An Effigy *and* Gravestone?

In the 1840s, the floor of the rotunda in the Temple Church was excavated. A row of medieval coffins was discovered between its two easternmost columns; these burials would have been right in front of the rotunda's altar and rood-screen. As was clear from the surviving bones, at least one of the knights would have stood over six feet tall – a giant in the 13th century, and all the more imposing on a war-horse. Here, almost certainly, were the bones of the tall, handsome, imposing William Marshal, Earl of Pembroke, 'the greatest knight of the world'.

Since 1843 one of the grand medieval effigies in the Temple Church has been identified as William's. Its face is of an old man; effigies generally show their subject in the prime of life, but William came to his greatest fame when in his 60s and 70s and may therefore have been purposely shown as the elderly Regent. The knight's sword pierces the head of a dragon; this is a rare effigial motif, but it matches the sword and dragon on King John's effigy in Worcester Cathedral. William had remained conspicuously loyal to John, and his family may have wanted to emphasize that loyalty.

So far, so good. But we have a loose end to tie up. In 1594, an antiquary wrote about the Temple Church memorials. On one he had read the inscriptions *Comes Penbrochiae* (Earl of Pembroke) and *Miles eram Martis Mars multos vicerat armis* (I was a soldier of Mars, the god of war; Mars had defeated many with [my] weapons). Later antiquaries identified this as the memorial of the great William Marshal. None of the surviving memorials has any such inscription. Either the inscription has been erased or the memorial unaccountably destroyed.

LEFT The effigies of William Marshal I and (beyond) of William Marshal II, today, in the Rotunda of the Temple Church.

RIGHT The newly discovered drawing, c. 1610, of a gravestone, perhaps of William Marshal.

FAR RIGHT The effigy believed to be of William Marshal: before the Church was bombed in 1941.

A set of drawings by John Guillim, c. 1610, has now been discovered in the Folger Shakespeare Library, Washington, DC. They depict all the Temple Church effigies. They also show a gravestone which bears a lion rampant (the Marshals' arms) and part of the antiquaries' inscription. The gravestone had disappeared by the 1730s.

The inscription's grand military claim is certainly better suited to William than to any of his sons. The drawing raises a fascinating question: have we got a glimpse at last of William's own gravestone?

WILLIAM MARES THE ELDER
EARL OF PEMBROKE

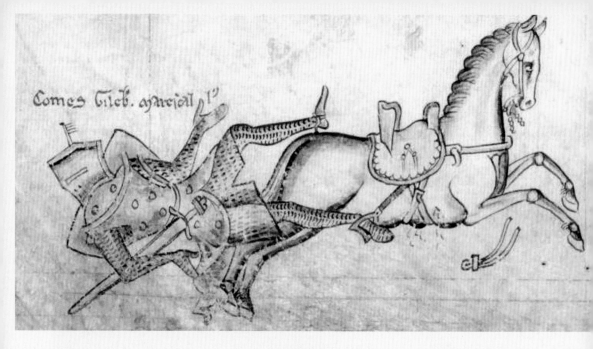

Comes Gileb. ajmejal. p̄.

FIVE DEATHS IN FIFTEEN YEARS
The End of the Dynasty

William had vast interests to protect in Ireland. He made powerful enemies there, not least Ailbe (Albinus), Bishop of Ferns, who claimed that William had refused to return some of the Bishop's lands. All William's sons died without legitimate issue; a story spread that the Bishop had cursed William and so brought about the end of his dynasty.

William Marshal II had been one of the twenty-five Surety Barons, charged with ensuring King John's conformity to the demands of Magna Carta; he and his father, then, had cannily divided their loyalties between John and the barons. By spring 1217 he was back on the side of his father and of Henry III. He married Eleanor, the sister of Henry III, but he died suddenly in 1231 and was buried in the Temple Church. His effigy now lies beside his father's.

The earldom passed to his younger brother Richard, who rebelled against Henry III in Wales and was then trapped and killed by the king's justiciar in Ireland. So to the next brother Gilbert, who had launched on a career in the Church; in 1241 he was killed in a tournament, where he was surely hoping to emulate his father's success but lacked all his father's legendary skills. He was thrown by his horse, his foot got stuck in the stirrup, and he was fatally dragged along the ground. His effigy in the Temple Church shows a dragon biting a strap on his foot.

The two remaining brothers, Walter and Ancel, then died within a month of each other in 1245. Less than thirty years after William's

own death, the Marshal dynasty of male descendants had come to an end.

However, his daughters flourished. Of his five daughters, he married Maud, the eldest, to Sir Hugh Bigod, who became 3rd Earl of Norfolk on his father's death in 1221. The Duke of Norfolk is still, to this day, the hereditary Earl Marshal of England. Isabel married Gilbert de Clare, Earl of Hertford and Gloucester, and Sibyl married William de Ferrers, who became 5th Earl of Derby on his father's death. Children and grandchildren followed; William Marshal's descendants are all around us.

LEFT The death of Gilbert Marshal in an illegal tournament, 1241.

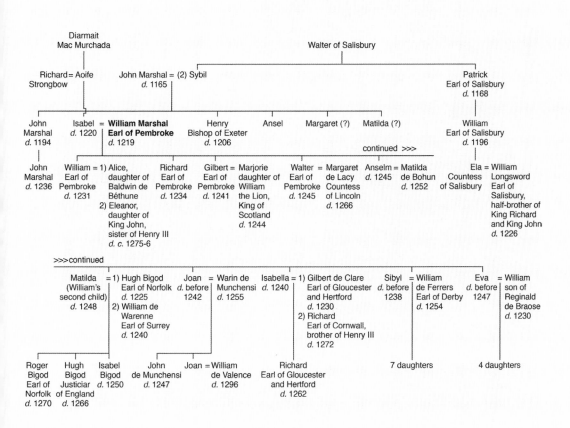

Diarmait Mac Murchada — Walter of Salisbury

Richard = Aoife Strongbow | John Marshal = (2) Sybil *d.* 1165 | Patrick Earl of Salisbury *d.* 1168

John Marshal *d.* 1194 | Isabel *d.* 1220 = **William Marshal Earl of Pembroke** *d.* 1219 | Henry Bishop of Exeter *d.* 1206 | Ansel | Margaret (?) | Matilda (?) | William Earl of Salisbury *d.* 1196

continued >>>

John Marshal *d.* 1236 | William Earl of Pembroke *d.* 1231 = 1) Alice, daughter of Baldwin de Béthune 2) Eleanor, daughter of King John, sister of Henry III *d. c.* 1275-6 | Richard Earl of Pembroke *d.* 1234 | Gilbert Earl of Pembroke *d.* 1241 = Marjorie daughter of William the Lion, King of Scotland *d.* 1244 | Walter Earl of Pembroke *d.* 1245 = Margaret de Lacy Countess of Lincoln *d.* 1266 | Anselm *d.* 1245 = Matilda de Bohun *d.* 1252 | Ela Countess of Salisbury = William Longsword Earl of Salisbury, half-brother of King Richard and King John *d.* 1226

>>>continued

Matilda (William's second child) *d.* 1248 = 1) Hugh Bigod Earl of Norfolk *d.* 1225 2) William de Warenne Earl of Surrey *d.* 1240 | Joan *d.* before 1242 = Warin de Munchensi *d.* 1255 | Isabella *d.* 1240 = 1) Gilbert de Clare Earl of Gloucester and Hertford *d.* 1230 2) Richard Earl of Cornwall, brother of Henry III *d.* 1272 | Sibyl *d.* before 1238 = William de Ferrers Earl of Derby *d.* 1254 | Eva *d.* before 1247 = William son of Reginald de Braose *d.* 1230

Roger Bigod Earl of Norfolk *d.* 1270 | Hugh Bigod Justiciar of England *d.* 1266 | Isabel Bigod *d.* 1250 | John de Munchensi *d.* 1247 | Joan = William de Valence *d.* 1296 | Richard Earl of Gloucester and Hertford *d.* 1262 | 7 daughters | 4 daughters

THE HISTORY OF *THE HISTORY*
An Amazing Discovery

Only one manuscript of *The History* is known – and that was lost for over 600 hundred years. Its rediscovery is a romance in itself. A young French scholar, Paul Meyer, saw it, catalogued simply as a 'Norman-French Chronicle on English Affairs (in Verse)' in an auction-sale at Sotheby's in 1861. Meyer had no idea what it was, but could instantly tell its importance. He tried to buy it for the French Bibliothèque Impériale, but was outbid by the wealthy and acquisitive Sir Thomas Phillipps.

For years Meyer searched for other references to this chronicle he had so briefly glanced at, and indeed to gain access to Phillipps' collection of 60,000 manuscripts. There were once at least three copies of the text: at Westminster Abbey, at St Augustine's Abbey at Canterbury and in the library of Thomas, Duke of Gloucester.

At last, after Phillipps' own death, his family allowed Meyer to look for the chronicle in Phillipps' collection. In 1881 Meyer, by then a scholar of international standing, found the manuscript that he had, for over twenty years, been looking for: over 19,000 lines of rhymed verse telling a story, as its own conclusion tells its readers, 'so remarkable it should be loved and enjoyed wherever it is heard.'

Within a year Meyer published a long introductory essay on his discovery. He tried, of course, to identify *The History*'s author. The younger William Marshal had commissioned it. The great William's long-standing and loyalist liegeman John of Earley had provided material for it. But who was the minstrel who transformed the story into thousands of lines of fine, rhymed verse? Perhaps – but not certainly – another 'John', mentioned in passing.

Meyer admitted that he was speculating when he wondered – just *wondered* – if two stories about William's early years were in fact disguised stories about *The History*'s author: as the young herald-at-arms, the singer to whom William gave the horse at Joigny, and as the so-called 'Henry the Northerner', the herald-at-arms who would cry out over the tournament fields, 'This way! Over here! God save the Marshal!'

It may not, in the end, be for the moments of high politics that we turn most keenly to *The History*, but for the rollicking stories of William's tournaments, the set-piece stories – sometimes funny, and happily told at William's own expense – of his ingenuous, impetuous courage, and for the consistency of 'the honest, guileless, modest Marshal' portrayed from the first line to the last.

This fearless fighter and politician was a man who saved both England and her Great Charter. We have good reason, 800 years on, to love and enjoy his story still.

LEFT The Rotunda of the Temple Church, London. The Marshals' effigies are on the right.

STILL REMEMBERED:
'The Loyalist Knight'

So said King Philip of France, on hearing of William's death. When William was dying, he described King John as a 'criminal ancestor' of Henry III. But William had remained loyal nonetheless, and so had saved England from anarchy.

Historians still wonder how reliable is *The History*'s account of William. It was commissioned by William's own eldest son, the younger William, who in 1224 married the King's sister. *The History* was written in 1224–26, when Henry III was securely on the throne. The great Earl had clearly to be presented in a glowing light; his loyalty to successive kings – and in particular to the young Henry III as a child – was to be a bright thread running through the story.

Events early in John's reign, on the other hand, could be left undescribed: the help given by William to the new king, and the great benefits bestowed on him by a grateful John. *The History* skirts as well around the events of 1214–15: Magna Carta is not even mentioned. About these years, 'this is', the author explains, 'no place to speak of the whys and wherefores of what went on; the truth is that neither party was innocent – anyone who hadn't seen it for himself would struggle to believe the wickedness committed by both sides. The war involved many things unworthy of record, and it might get me into trouble.' It might indeed; for his patron, the younger William, had sided

'a man of loyal and noble heart, no matter how he had been treated by the King, he could never be persuaded to forsake him.'

against the King with the barons and then with Louis of France.

Other moments might confuse us too when the rules of medieval fealty caused real conflicts of loyalty. William, we have seen, owed fealty for some lands to the King of France, and in their defence, remained loyal to him. Again, he owed fealty to Richard Lionheart for some possessions, to John for others, and he was hard pushed to explain to either why at some moments he was loyal to the other.

The History parades William's determination to observe his oaths, and indeed he could probably claim that wherever he had sworn fealty or allegiance, he had never reneged. All his prowess, courage, skills and influence would be at his liege-lord's use. In an age of ever-shifting loyalties, he was a man who could be trusted. And when it most mattered, in 1214–17, he was the one fixed point around which all the other protagonists could constellate, quite sure of where he stood.

'The Marshal at least,' *The History* tells us, 'a man of loyal and noble heart, stayed with King John in hard and difficult circumstances. He never left him, until the day he died, and I declare he stayed with his followers even then. It's a proven fact, very often observed, that, no matter how he had been treated by the King, he could never be persuaded to forsake him.' That loyalty saved King John; and it saved England.